MELODY

SIKU'S
Song

By Julia Jordan Kamanda

Illustrated by Sita DeGiulio Das

Bird By Julia Books
a division of J3Music Studios
Lancaster, PA

Dedicated to my mom and dad, who have always encouraged me to sing the songs that bubble up from my heart. —J.J.K.

To my husband Dijesh; I love all your songs! —S.D.D.

This project would not have been possible without the support of some very special people. Thank you (again) to Nancy and Scott Silverstein, Stanley Jordan, David Jordan, Luis Alvarez, Sallie Bengtson, and Hope and Les Law. Linda Amesquita and the Amesquita family, thank you for sharing the beautiful Peruvian textiles that are used in the artwork. To all—your love is in each and every one of these pages.—The Musical Tales team

ISBN 978-0-9907851-1-8

Published by Bird By Julia Books, a division of J3 Music Studios, LLC.

www.J3MusicStudios.com/BirdByJuliaBooks

Bird By Julia Books
Lancaster, PA

Printed in the United States of America

Executive Editor: Sandra Kilpatrick Jordan
Book Design: R studio T
This book was typeset in Jacoby Black and Myanmar Regular.
The illustrations were rendered in mixed media and digitally.

AUDIO TRACKS
"Siku's Song Audiobook"
Recorded, mixed, and mastered by John LeVasseur-Sound Design Music Studio
Performed by Julia Jordan Kamanda, narrator; Cienna Kamanda, Siku's voice.

"In My Heart (There Is a Song)" words and music by Julia Jordan Kamanda
Mixed and mastered by John LeVasseur-Sound Design Music Studio
Performed by Julia Jordan Kamanda, vocals; Crosby Renninger, Alexandria Fernandez, Riley Fidler, Sophia Subacz, background vocals.

"Pan Flute Party"
Mastered by John LeVasseur-Sound Design Music Studio
Recorded by Julia Jordan Kamanda using audio loops from Apple Logic Pro

Library of Congress Control Number: 2015906169

Note to Parents and Teachers

Siku's Song explores the musical element of MELODY, which is a string of notes that you can sing with words or hum without words. Think of melody as the voice of the song that climbs up and down. This story includes particular melodies as shown in the notes provided below. Wherever you see this symbol:

sing the melody that is written with it, or play it on a pan flute or piano.

New to music notation? Learn these simple melodies by listening to the example tracks on the CD provided with the storybook.

ex. 1: FAMILY SONG

ex. 2: WAY UP HIGH

ex. 3: WAY DOWN LOW

ex. 4:
WAY UP HIGH THEN
DOWN LOW

ex. 5: PAN FLUTE SONG

ex. 6: SIKU'S SONG

Siku was a young alpaca who lived a long time ago in the shadow of the Andes mountains. In her early days, she learned to stand, and run, and jump in the deep green valley where all alpacas lived. And in those busy days, Siku also learned to sing her Family Song.

ex. 1

Siku sang whenever she felt the music bubble up from her heart. She sang when she was hungry. She sang when she was tired. She sang when she was happy, and when she was sad.

Sometimes she would sing way up high.

Sometimes Siku would sing way down low.

ex. 3

Sometimes she would sing way up high, then way down low again.

ex. 4

And sometimes Siku would sing the Family Song as loudly as she could.

ex. 1

Sometimes her parents smiled, but sometimes they frowned. "That Siku sure loves to sing loudly," they worried to each other.

In Siku's time, alpacas believed that their elders' ears were made of glass. They believed that singing loud notes might shatter their ears to pieces. So because they could be just a bit quieter, alpacas became experts at humming.

All the alpacas in the valley were bound by the same rule: they were only allowed to sing their own Family Song with no loud notes.

Siku practiced singing and humming, just like she practiced running and jumping in the deep green valley.

ex. 1

One day, Siku heard a new song coming from the hills.
A woman on the walking path was playing a beautiful melody.

ex. 5

Siku heard this new song flow gently over her little body. She listened, and she sang along.

ex. 5

She listened, and she sang along again.

ex. 5

And then more notes began to bubble up from her heart.
She sang until she finally came to her own melody.

ex. 6

It was so beautiful. It was so perfect. Siku raced back home to share it. "Mom! Dad!" she cried. "Listen to my new song!"

ex. 6

Her father said
sternly, "Siku, have
you not listened
to the Alpaca
Singing Rule? We
must only sing the
Family Song. What
I have said is final."

"Our song is so boring, daddy!" Siku cried. "I want to sing my own songs, the songs that bubble up from my heart!" She begged and pleaded with her parents to let her sing her own songs. But they said no.

Siku was mad! "Why do we even have this rule? she yelled. "Shhhh, Siku. This is the melody we have *hummed* for many generations," explained her father. "This is the melody we will continue to hum for many generations to come. Have you forgotten? We don't want to shatter our elder's ears of glass."

Siku ran to the edge of the valley. She did not know what to do, so she sang. Her song drifted through the mountains to the elder's special resting place.

ex. 6

"Siku, that was beautiful!" said Elder Mama, lying in the shade of a eucalyptus tree. "From your first days, my child, I have heard you sing. You have a gift that must be shared with others."

Mama stood, and everyone sat in silence to listen to her words. "On behalf of all the elders, I decree that from this moment forward, all alpacas may sing the songs that bubble up from their hearts." The elders nodded in agreement.

"But," Elder Mama continued, "We do ask that all alpacas *hum* their songs, so as not to shatter our ears of glass."

Siku turned to see her father beaming with pride. "Sometimes it just takes one little voice to make a big change. Thank you for sharing your song with us. Will you teach it to me?"

From that day on, all alpacas were free to sing the melodies that bubbled up from their hearts. Siku and her family sang and hummed all kinds of songs, but their favorite was Siku's Song. It was a song that was meant for everyone — even the elders.

ex. 6